SHARE MY LONESOME VALLEY

The Slow Grief Of Long-term Care

by

Doug Manning

In-Sight Books

2nd printing–November 2001

Copyright© 1999 by In-Sight Books, Inc.
P. O. Box 42467
Oklahoma City, Oklahoma 73123
1-800-658-9262
www.insightbooks.com

Manufactured in the United States of America

ISBN 1-892785-33-1

To
Chuck and Suky Pollard,
Terry Elder,
and
The Support Network
in
Naples, Florida

INDEX

Section I
Nobody Knows My Pain

Section II
The Grieving Process

Section III
Facing The Future

Section IV

Section I

Nobody Knows My Pain

Suffering in silence
is
highly over-rated

Chapter I

The Lonesome Valley

As soon as they came into the room it was evident they were accustomed to being important. It was more than the clothes she wore, or the care she had been able to lavish on herself. There was an air about them that let you know they were more than just the people next door. She pushed his wheel chair up to a table and started gathering their coffee and rolls before the seminar began. Her husband could best be described as an imposing person. In spite of the effects of Alzheimer's, he still looked brilliant and powerful. When I introduced myself to them, she responded graciously and seemed genuinely appreciative. She walked me off to the side so her husband could not hear and said, "My husband started seven major companies. We were personal friends of President and Mrs. Reagan and have spent many nights in the White House. Now he has Alzheimer's disease and my heart just breaks for him."

I must admit that I missed hearing what I should have heard. I was so intrigued with the man, so curious about what companies he owned, and so taken with their frequent visits to the White House that I totally missed what she wanted me to hear. We talked about the businesses, and he had owned some very well-known large corporations. We talked about the Reagans and their close relationship. We talked about how ironic it was that both her husband and President Reagan have developed Alzheimer's disease. We talked about how horrible this disease is and how it robs brilliant people of everything they hold dear. We talked about how hard it is to see someone like her husband die by small degrees or millimeters at a time. We covered every aspect of what was happening to her husband—BUT we never talked about HER.

What about her losses? What about her pain? What about her grief? As she was telling me about her husband, she was also crying out for someone to notice her pain. Finding a way to communicate the inner pain we feel when a mate has such a debilitating disease is difficult. How can you stand next to the wheel chair of a former titan of industry, who is in the advanced stages of Alzheimer's Disease, and talk about anything except his pain? Isn't that selfish? Won't it sound silly? How could your little pains even be mentioned in the same room, much less the same breath, as the losses sitting right in front of us?

But it is neither selfish nor is it silly. She may not have consciously known it but she was really saying, "LOOK AT WHAT I HAVE LOST!

See how my life has been turned upside down.
How can one go from luxury to nursemaid in
such a short time? How do you live through
losing your husband while his body is still alive?
How do you survive the slow grief of thousands
of small sorrows? How do you stand seeing this
person, who was the strength of my life, shrivel
into someone who can't drink his own coffee?
Tell me how you do that and still smile for the
world to see? Tell me how you do that and
never let anyone hear a complaint? And yet,
because his pain is so great, these issues and
my pain are not important, not spoken, and not
heard."

I could tell a thousand stories just like this
one. I hear them all over the world. The
diseases change, but the experiences of being
dominated by the demands of care remain
constant in each of the stories. The moment a
loved one is diagnosed with such diseases as
Alzheimer's, AIDS, Parkinson's, cancer, ALS,
stroke, chronic depression or other emotional
illnesses, and the list could go on, your name
changes to caregiver. From that moment your
life is dominated by that title.

Just as there are many kinds of long-term
diseases, there are many different levels of
caregiving. You may be a spouse doing full-time
care for a mate in your home. You may have
already given care for several years, or you may

be in those frightening early days of denying the diagnosis.

You may be a child giving care, either in your home or the home of your parent. In either case your role has changed completely. Your home has been lost for the duration of the care.

You may be caring for a loved one in a health care setting such as a hospital or nursing home. If so, you now spend your time walking halls and begging for more information.

Or, you may find yourself trying to give care from a distance. Your work demands that you live many miles from home and now your parents are in need. Your life is dominated by making phone calls to arrange for care, checking on conditions, or dreading to hear the phone ring for fear of the possible bad news. You spend every day off and vacation time making trips back home. Your work suffers, your home life suffers, and you still feel guilty for not doing more and being there more often. You face decisions about care that have no solid answers. The fact that you are not there in person providing care every day does not lessen the domination, nor the grief and pain.

It sounds impossible, but long-term care sneaks up on us. The need for care grows so gradually that we do not notice how much of our life is being controlled and dominated by the caregiving. Before we realize it, there is a hospital bed in the living room and oxygen tanks by the television. We are either giving care, or thinking about giving care, twenty-four hours a day. That has been called by authors Nancy Mace and Peter Rabins *"The Thirty Six Hour Day."* The Thirty Six Hour Day; Johns Hopkins Press, Baltimore, MD, 1991, Second Edition .

Families confronted with a sudden illness or a traumatic accident are much more likely to talk about what they are personally experiencing. They explain it in great detail at every opportunity. They are very aware of what they have lost. They are aware of how that loss is impacting their lives, and they tell the world.

Long-term care folks seem to just "function in the fire." I have heard that if a frog is placed in a pan of cold water and put on the stove, the frog's body adapts to the water as it heats and the frog will cook without jumping out of the pan. Many families are in situations that are gradually heating up, and, because the escalation has been so gradual, they have not noticed how much hot water they are in.

This book is written for caregivers. It does not talk about how to give care. It is not a manual on the decision making this care demands. The one focus of this book is you taking care of you. If your name is caregiver then you are dominated by the very disease you fight. Just as in the woman's story, you talk about your loved one, you talk about the disease and its progress and probably never notice what the disease and the care are doing to you and your world. If this book reaches its objective, you will have at least noticed.

Chapter II

Care For The Caregiver

A professor in a school of mines asked his class to name the most important thing to come out of the mines. They guessed gold, silver, diamonds and other valuable minerals. The professor said, "The most important thing to come out of the mines is the miner."

The most important issue you face as a caregiver of a long-term illness is you. If you don't take care of you–you will not give efficient care to your loved one over the long haul. If you don't take care of you–you will soon find yourself with no emotional strength to give and no feelings left to share. If you do not take care of you–the chances increase that you will precede your loved one in death.

Taking Care Of Yourself

Taking care of yourself while giving care to a loved one is far easier said than done. People will frequently tell you to take care of yourself, but few will have any plans for how you can accomplish this feat. It seems every moment of every day is filled, and every day brings a new crisis or task that must be added to an already full day. Then someone comes along to blithely say, "Take care of yourself." If you weren't so tired you might argue, but it would do no good and just take up energy you need for the next chore.

I cringe when I hear folks say, "God won't put more on you than you can bear". Folks who say that have not walked in your shoes. Anyone caring for an Alzheimer's patient, a loved one with cancer, or some other debilitating disease has "more than they can bear" and has it every day. Incidentally, that statement is not in the Bible. The Bible says we will not face a temptation we cannot escape from, but says nothing about our loads being so easily handled.

The physical exertion, plus the emotional strain, plus the feelings of fear and insecurity, plus the family pressures that are so often and so skillfully applied, can add up to more that anyone can bear. For that reason you must find some way to rest. Hard or not, impossible or not, there must be rest. There will not be a lot of chances to do so but you must take every opportunity offered and try to create as many as possible.

Often the problem is not the lack of opportunities, it may well be our reluctance to take advantage of the chances to rest that are available. I have been shocked to find how hard it is to get people to use the adult day care centers when they are available. I found a center in Florida that is built to care for Alzheimer's patients. The director told me their greatest struggle involved getting the families to take advantage of their services.

The same can be said for the Respite Care programs available in most nursing homes. These programs will care for a loved one a week or so at a time to give the caregiver a break. These valuable chances for rest are sparsely used.

There seems to be some kind of stigma attached to not caring for the loved one 100% of the time. To "put them in one of those places" seems to say we don't love them like we should. Often I get the feeling we are afraid of how it will look to some mythical body of judges who watch how we give care and somehow tell the world the score. It is very easy to become paranoid when we are the caregiver.

So, instead of taking time off, we make excuses for not resting. I hear, "I can't take off right now, maybe soon." Which really means never. "My loved one is not feeling well right now." The loved one is never feeling well enough for us to rest. We must force ourselves to take time off for their good and for our own health and sanity.

"What if something happens while I am gone?" Something may happen while you are gone. That is a fact. My father-in-law died while my wife and her mother were on a much needed trip. There was guilt for a while, but we realized that the outcome would have been the same if they had been right by his bedside.

I think it is important to realize that rest must include time away. As long as we are there, the problems and the pressures remain on our shoulders. A week-end away can do wonders for our spirits and our energy.

Proper Diet

Far too often we get so caught up in giving care that we forget to watch our own diet. We wind up eating fast food more often than we cook. We "grab something" on the run and promise ourselves a better meal next time. The next time never comes. Giving care is the equivalent of hard manual labor. It has the same effect as laying bricks or running a jack hammer all day. It does not seem to be that strenuous, but the energy needed is far beyond what we can muster on a poor diet.

A Time For You

Snatch a little time for yourself any time you can. The dishes may not get done before company comes or the beds may not be made every day, but you need those little times of quiet when you can relax, think and recharge your batteries. Beds made don't matter nearly as much as minds recharged and spirits revived.

Freedom To Feel And Say It

You have the right to complain. You have the right to tell the world that you got the raw end of the stick. There is no value in suffering in silence. There is no virtue in being a martyr. Too often we think we are suppose to take life's traumatic events in stride and make some heroic statement about how good it feels to do so. It doesn't feel good and we should not accept any pressure to say it does. We need the freedom to feel what we feel. We cannot change these feelings by suppressing them away.

We need to be able to admit to ourselves, "Today I really feel alone, or afraid, or forsaken, or angry". We have a right to feel the feelings that are there. We also have the right to talk about those same feelings to others. That is not being weak, nor does it show a lack of faith, nor a lack of love for the patient.

I express it in a rather crude manner when I say, "We have to keep our 'Cussing' current". Don't let it build up. That does not mean we must use bad words. There are some wonderful ways of letting off steam with words that are not offensive to anyone. There are times when we just need to lean back and let it all out. Say it with gusto and feel better.

Isn't That Selfish?

On the surface this whole chapter sounds selfish. It sounds as if you are to play "poor me" games and whine a lot. Or that you are to think only about yourself while your loved one suffers. Isn't that total selfishness? There is a vast difference between selfishness and survival. When dealing with this kind of intense stress, we need to give ourselves permission to survive. That is not selfish–it's just plain smart.

Chapter III

Barriers To Caring

Finding the time to take care of ourselves is most difficult. Finding the energy to do so may be even harder. Many of us have other forces that drive us to provide care until we have driven ourselves into the ground. Before we can begin to find ways of accepting care for ourselves we must take an honest, and sometimes painful, look at the forces that drive us.

If you are the one who provides the care while other members of the family do very little, it would be wise to explore how that happened. Most families will try to hang it on one person and, far too often, they then feel free to sit back and criticize every decision and action the designated person makes. This person becomes the primary caregiver. Everywhere I go I meet people who are trapped into those situations and have no idea how or when it happened.

Of course, some primary caregivers are spouses or partners and the job fell on their shoulders as a natural response to need. Some others became the primary caregiver because they lived near the parents and started helping out when one of the parents needed help caring for the other parent. Gradually the caregiving parent also needed care and the helping child inherited the job. Even those who inherited the task through these natural causes need to be careful about how driven they become in giving care.

The Unblessed Child

Often the job is accepted in an effort to earn the parent's love. Many have what I call the "Unblessed Child Syndrome." It is amazing how many families have at least one child who does not feel blessed. They don't think they are as talented, or attractive, or as intelligent as the other children. Most don't feel they have ever lived up to their parent's expectations for them. Many only children feel unblessed.

Some unblessed children leave home and never return but most never leave home. They stay close and spend their lives trying to earn the blessing. I know fifty-five-year-old women who go visit their mothers four times a day and, every time they go, their mother tells them how great the other kids are—never how great they are. A woman told me she had never bought a gift that her mother had acknowledged. She had, at last, found the perfect gift. It was far too expensive but she put it in lay-a-way for Christmas. She spent six months paying for that gift. When she presented the gift, her mother never said a word. This woman has a sister whose gift to their mother was a handkerchief. The mother put the handkerchief in a frame and hung it on the wall. Every time anyone comes by, her mother points and says, "See what Ellen sent me."

That same lady cried in my office and said, "I can tell Mother to wear her boots when she goes out in the cold and she will never hear me. My sister could tell her to burn the house down and Mother would set it on fire immediately." That describes the unblessed child syndrome.

It is amazing how often the unblessed child becomes the primary caregiver for the parents. It is logical because most still live near their parent's home. If they have moved away they will move back. Even if an unblessed child leaves physically they never leave emotionally. At the first sign of need, they are there.

It is also logical because the unblessed child sees this as their opportunity to finally be loved. They think they can give care and be accepted at last. If this is a picture of you–don't count on it working.

It is not just the parents that put the pressure on the caregiver. Sometimes it is the other siblings. A woman told of having full responsibility for her mother. Her sister lived in the same city and did not have to work. This lady had to work and still give the care. The sister did not help in any manner, not even financially. One year she was so far behind in her work that she asked her sister to take their mother for two weeks so she could get caught up, After one week, the sister called and said, "You've got to come get this woman. She is driving me insane!"

When the woman arrived to pick up the mother, her sister met her on the front porch and said, "Don't you dare put my mother in a nursing home."

I asked that woman what I ask unblessed children around the world. Why do you let people do that to you? No one can put that kind of guilt on you without your permission. Manipulation is by invitation only. Why do you allow it?

The only answer for the unblessed child is to stand and say, "This is me. You decide whether or not you want to love me just as I am. If so, great. If not, I will live without it. I am not going to spend my life chasing a rainbow that has no pot of gold at the end."

I was the unblessed child in my home. There came a day when I was able to no longer care whether or not my parents loved me. After that I was able to build a great relationship with them.

The Search For Normal Feelings

Some of us are driven by a deep sense of guilt because of the way we feel. One of the real problems in long-term care is that we do not know how we are suppose to feel. We don't know what is <u>normal</u>. If I have a calling in life it is to go around telling people that they are normal. Most of us don't know that we are. We think we feel things no one else feels or that we don't feel things everyone else feels. No one knows what others feel so we just decide their feelings must be very different than ours.

One woman told me she was going to hug my neck and then tell me why she did it. She said her mother was in one wing of the nursing home with Alzheimer's disease and her husband was in another wing of the same nursing home with the same disease. She said, "You are the first person to come along and say it was all right to be angry about that." Then she took me to where the two wings met and said, "That is my spot. I have stood right there many a night and cussed them both. Then I go home and think I must be the only person in the world that ever felt that way about a mother and husband who had Alzheimer's." But she isn't. We love them but we still get tired. We still get angry. We still get frustrated. We love them but still there are times when we just wish it was over. We feel burdened and then feel guilty because we feel burdened. These are normal feelings.

If we don't know what normal is we tend to become Overcompensators. Overcompensators are people who can't feel good about how they feel inside so they try to make things more than perfect on the outside. They kill themselves in caring. They never can find anyone they can trust to give care so they must do it all themselves. Even while they work, they still feel horribly guilty because they don't think they feel what they are suppose to feel, or they don't feel it deeply enough.

Far too often we are driven by some fear of what others might think. The most feared people in the world are a people called "THEY." We worry about what "they" think or what "they" will say. The strange thing is we don't even know who "they" are. Who are these folks that govern our very lives? Who is it that might think we are not good mates or children? Who is it that watches us like hawks to find every mistake we might be guilty of? The minute you take on the care of a loved one is the moment you need to tell the rest of the world to go mind their own business. You have far too much on your plate to worry about what some busy body says or thinks. This is the time to get free of all of that burden.

Caregiver Syndrome

Some of us have what I call the "Caregiver Syndrome." This syndrome means we know how to give care, but we don't know how to receive care. We get very good at giving love and never learn how to be loved. I have caregiver syndrome. I will sit up with a person and listen to their pain all night if necessary. But if I sat there all night they would never know of my pain, because I would not tell them. That is caregiver syndrome. Those of us so afflicted get all of our jollies out of giving care. We love to hear that we are doing too much. That is like saying "sic-em" to a bull dog. We will work that much harder so someone might say it again. We are not trying to be martyrs, we just get most of our worth out of giving beyond the call.

We use our giving as a form of control. If someone says, "I am sorry your brother died," I immediately say, "Thanks, but tell me how are you?" I must be the healer, I can't be the healee. I must be the blesser, I can't be the blessee. The results are obvious. We work ourselves into the ground in giving and serving. We can't take time off. We can't allow others to help. We can't take even a short break. All we know is how to serve.

When my brother died I was in Atlanta. He died on Tuesday afternoon and I was on the phone with his family when he passed away.

That was about 2:30 p.m. Atlanta time. I had to make a speech at 4:00 and another at 7:30. I made them both and no one ever knew. I went out to dinner with the host between the speeches and never said a word about my brother's dying. That is caregiver syndrome. I didn't want them to try to comfort me. All I knew was how to comfort, not how to be comforted.

I had planned to stay in Atlanta until Thursday in order to be interviewed on CNN. It never crossed my mind to change those plans. I made the flight arrangements to do the interview on Thursday morning, catch a plane that afternoon and meet my wife and my mother in California for the funeral. I went to bed that night with all plans in place. I woke up in the night realizing that I no longer wanted to be strong. I wanted to go home. I wanted to cry and have someone comfort me. I caught the first plane home the next morning. That is the healthiest day of my life. I invite you to join me in my new found health. It is not enough to know how to love. It is only enough when we know how to be loved in return.

Chapter IV

A Collection Of Quiet Sorrows

Grief is the natural response to any loss. Anytime there is a loss we experience grief. Losing a billfold leaves a hollow place in the pit of your stomach. That hollow feeling is a form of grief. The grief we experience in long-term care of a terminally ill loved one differs from the grief following a death, but it is part of the same process. When we experience the death of a loved one an overwhelming blast of loss and grief envelopes us. When we are providing care through a long-term illness we experience a collection of quiet sorrows that accumulate over time until they eventually overwhelm us. Because the build–up of the grief is gradual and slowly accumulating, we may not recognize nor acknowledge that we are in grief. One quiet sorrow builds on another quiet sorrow and, before we even notice it, we are engulfed.

Unacknowledged quiet sorrows can gradually leave us emotionally drained. There is a form of depression that does not cause blue or sad feelings. This depression results in no feelings at all. We become emotionally flat. We seem to be detached from our own bodies. It is as though we are standing off to the side watching ourselves go through the motions and do our duties, but we do not feel any connection. We function, but we do not want to function. We give care, but the feelings we once experienced when we gave care have vanished.

All of us have days when we feel emotionally flat. Days when we cannot awaken feelings of care about anything. That is normal. If those feelings persist over time we need to notice and respond. Long time detachment is a red flag that says we are on the edge of being overwhelmed. We need a break. We need to talk to a friend. We may need to let off steam or even explode about how we feel. It might help to go see a funny movie. Laughter allows us to let go of buried feelings.

Another symptom of being overwhelmed is a loss of energy. We are tired and cannot seem to get rested. No matter what we do, the tiredness doesn't leave. Our energy levels are connected to our emotional gas tank and when one goes the other is affected. Loss of energy should also be a red flag warning us to take a close look at ourselves.

Some people lose their sense of humor. Things you once did not even notice now hurt your feelings. You begin to make mountains out of molehills and then climb the mountains to count each rock.

Or we might just develop a constant state of being half-mad at the whole world. All of us have days when we don't like anyone. Days when we think everyone else is only out for themselves and no one cares about us. A day or so of this is normal. A week or so of this means we need to give ourselves some tender loving care. Attending to our needs is the only way to have the stamina and emotional strength to care for others.

Sharing The Quiet Sorrows

I have asked people who were involved in the experience of long-term care to list these quiet, and often hidden, sorrows. Maybe reading a list will help you think of your collection of unnoticed losses. Space will be provided for you to add yours to the list. What have you lost? The answer given most frequently was:

We lost the person before we lost the body. This is especially true when dementia is present. It can also be true in long-term illnesses like cancer or AIDS when medications change the personality or dull the senses until the person we knew and loved is no longer with us. The body is there as a constant reminder of our loss, but it is as if our loved one left long ago. Diseases like Lou Gehrig's or Parkinson's trap the mind in a body that no longer functions which makes it even more cruel that communication is no longer an option.

Even though the person we knew is gone, we have no process or method for grieving the departure. How do we express our sorrow when the body is still alive? Most of the time we handle it like the woman in Chapter One. We talk about what our loved one is going through and hope that makes us feel better.

Other responses were:

I lost companionship. Often every aspect of companionship is lost. Those long talks we once had. The warm sense of knowing someone who loves us is in the next room. The security we felt because we had each other. The help in making decisions. The mutual support we gave and received. Or, the wisdom we received from a parent. The sense of never having to feel alone, never having to be alone. Each of these must be grieved as they are lost.

I lost time. Every hour of every day is dominated by the disease. There is no time left for me. The quality of my loved one's life is gone, but so is mine.

I lost communication. Once we could talk about anything, now everything is strained. Once we could have a good head-clearing fight, now we act overly polite. Once we talked about our mutual interests, now we talk about doctor's visits, medication and how much pain my loved one feels. When communication is lost, the real basis of our life and relationship together is almost gone.

When the roles change between us we lose the ability to communicate and we must rebuild it. That can be demonstrated in any nursing home. A family can't stay in the room with their loved one for more than three minutes, but they can go next door and visit all afternoon with a stranger.

When I became "parent" to my father we went from being the very best of friends to being strangers. I felt on edge when he was around and did not know what to say. He stopped coming to my house unless it was a necessity. I felt a great deal of guilt. I thought I had stopped loving my own father. I finally confronted Dad with how I felt and found out that he did not like me either. He was losing control of his life and he decided I was somehow to blame.

When a spouse suddenly must take control of the things that once were the domain of the partner, communication must be reborn. It takes some confrontation and struggle but communication can be reborn. When children become "parent" to their parents, they experience some of the same struggle my father and I had to work through.

No matter how logical all this sounds, the end result is that we add the loss of communication to our list of quiet sorrows.

I lost my friends. They don't know what to say and seem uncomfortable if I am around. I am far too busy to call or go see them and somehow they drop away one by one. Each one adds another quiet sorrow to my pile. Late in the nights I lie awake and wonder what they are doing and if they miss me. Why can't they be more helpful and supportive when a friend is in pain?

I lost the mutual support and the help in making decisions. Now I must make medical decisions with so little knowledge and information, it's as though I'm playing "pin the tail on the donkey". I just close my eyes and hope I am doing the right thing. I try to find out more but, when the doctor gets through talking, I am more confused than ever. I ask others for help and support, and they try. But, when decision time comes, it is all me and my blindfolded choosing.

I lost my history. My spouse is in the advanced stages of Alzheimer's. I have no one to share memories with. I look back on our lives and see so many wonderful experiences we shared together. The best part of building memories is getting to look back and relive them together. What good is a memory you have to remember alone?

I can't express my loss in one word. Often the losses are more general in nature. Often we feel the loss of our attitudes and our responses to life. These folks say such things as "I have lost my zest for life, my fun, my passion, my stimulation." All of these seem to be in one package. All of them seem to be gone.

Hopefully this list has started the thinking process about your quiet sorrows. I am leaving room for you to add to the list or, lay the book aside, and write them out on separate paper. It will be helpful if you can get them in mind before we begin to talk about methods for dealing with them. The sorrows may be small, they may be quiet, but they are very important.

MY QUIET SORROWS

Section II

The Grieving Process

The large sorrows hit us out in the open
and
we are well aware of the effect on our lives.

The small sorrows creep in unaware
and
silently collect in the bottom of our soul.

Chapter V

The Grieving Process

A woman said her eight-year-old daughter's best friend had died and she had not told her daughter about the death. When I asked why she said, "If she knows, won't she grieve?" I said, "If you are lucky she will." Grief is not an enemy to be avoided. It is a process to be walked through. Grief is nature's way of healing a broken heart. We seem to have it all backwards. We think the best thing we can do is avoid grief. Let time heal. All of my life I have heard the phrase, "Time heals all wounds". In truth, time alone does very little healing. Waiting for time to heal is another way of saying the best way to handle grief is to ignore and internalize the pain. The best thing to do with grief is grieve. We grieve our way through the process toward healing.

This process takes a much longer time than we expect. I think it takes at least two years to walk through a loss. That does not mean we will hurt every day for two years. Nor does it mean that if someone is not "Well" in two years there is something wrong with them. We don't really ever "Get Well" after a loss. A chunk has been bitten out of our hearts and it will not grow back. We <u>can</u> turn the corner in the way we cope.

Most grief authors talk about the stages in grief. I listed four stages in my first book. I did not like the word "stage" then and I like it even less now. Stages seem like clear cut lines of demarcation—like stairs that we step up to one while leaving the other. Grief is not clear cut, nor do people go through it with any set pattern. Grief is as unique as a finger print. Everyone grieves in their own way and on their own schedule. There are no set clear cut steps to grief. We vacillate through the stages. We can be in stage two this morning and back to stage one this afternoon. I believe we can be in two stages at the same time.

I have searched for another analogy to describe grief. The best definition I know is that grief is like peeling an onion. It comes off one layer at a time and you cry a lot.

I love that analogy because it allows for flexibility. If 100 people were given onions, no one would have an onion exactly like anyone else's onion. If the people were instructed to peel the onion, everyone would do so in a different way. Each one would peel the onion in a way that suited their personalities. Some would play with the little peak at the top of the onion. Some would play with the little roots at the bottom. Some would tear into the onion with a vengeance. Others would peel it so daintily it would take them all day.

That is the picture of grief. There are some periods we can define, but we cannot tell the exact order nor the length of time any person will be involved in each period. Peeling an onion is a good picture of the grieving process.

Layer One—The Whirl

The outside of an onion is dry and crumbly. If crushed in the hand it can become confetti. If you do that to the outside of an onion and throw it in the air, you have demonstrated the first period of grief. It is a whirl. Ten thousand questions are up in the air, but none land long enough for us to ask them. Reality flashes by our minds but it is gone before we can focus on its impact. It is a period of shock and unreality. It seems real, and yet, it just can't have happened. A mother said, "I know we are planning a funeral for my son, but I expect that door will open any minute now and he will walk in and this nightmare will be over."

During this time we cry and hurt, but the awful reality of our loss has not yet hit. The reality will gradually dawn over the next days and weeks.

Layer Two—Reality

Gradually the whirl stops and the reality lands. This is the toughest time. We can't sleep, our chest hurts, we cry until we think there can't be another tear in our bodies, and then the tears start flowing even stronger. We call friends and can't remember what we were going to say. There are no short cuts through this period. We must walk through it. There is no way around it. We can deaden it with medications or alcohol, but when the deadening wears off, the pain is still there waiting for us.

We actually are doing the best job with grief when we are grieving. Grief has periods of intensity and then periods of rest. It comes in waves or grief bursts. When a burst hits we think we cannot survive the pain, and then, just as suddenly, there comes a time of release. It is during the burst that we are dealing with the feelings and doing the work of grief. If we can find the freedom and give ourselves permission to let our feelings flow then we will have taken some very valuable steps in walking through our grief.

Layer Three—Reaction

The reality period does not last for an extended period of time. This is partially true because we cannot stand it long-term. Something has to give. Our minds are wonderful at protecting us from overload. In grief we begin to move from reality to reaction and the motivating force behind this move is

anger. There is anger in grief. Since anger is a
normal reaction to hurt, it is logical that anger
should be present in this the deepest hurt of
life. Anger is healthy. Basically, we hit bottom,
get mad, and start fighting our way back.

Most people do not recognize the anger they
feel. We are not comfortable with that word. We
were raised thinking anger is wrong. We tend to
think anger is a synonym for hate, but they are
not the same. Because of our discomfort, we
have developed substitute words to use instead
of anger. We say we are not angry we are just
hurt, or frustrated, or depressed. My favorite is,
"I am not angry I am just UPSET." All of these
feelings come from the same basic emotion as
anger, so, for this study, let's just say we get
angry.

Even though the anger is healthy, we still
need to do something with the feelings as they
surface. If we swallow anger we end up
depressed. Most depression comes from
internalized anger. Often it helps to have some
physical way to work off this steam. I know a
woman who buys all the cheap dishes she can
find at garage sales. When she needs to vent
she breaks the dishes into the garbage
dumpster near her home. I am involved with a
children's grief center that has an "Emotion
Commotion" room. It is a sound-proof room
where the kids can punch a bag, throw things,

and scream until they find relief and peace. We all need just such a place where our anger can flow free.

The problem with anger is it doesn't float well. It needs to focus somewhere. It is not enough to be angry, we need to be angry at someone or something. The anger of grief will focus somewhere. Where it focuses is important. Often it focuses in places that seem to be unhealthy, but they aren't. They may be inconvenient but they aren't necessarily bad places to focus.

Sometimes the anger focuses irrationally. It is not unusual for a widow, for example, to get angry at her husband for dying. He might not have been able to do much about it, but it is amazing how many widows relate standing in a room and screaming, "Why did you leave me like this?" Afterwards they think they have lost their minds.

Some people get angry with God. Even though that scares the ministers to death, it really isn't a bad place for our anger to focus. God is big enough to handle our anger. God is loving enough to understand our feelings and accepting enough for us to tell Him to His face. Unfortunately, when we are angry with God there are very few people who will let us express it. They panic and feel they must protect the faith. This forces us to defend our feelings instead of expressing them. We end up denying and burying the feelings we most need to express.

Many get mad at physicians. Many of the lawsuits against physicians come out of the anger families feel. They were frustrated during the illness because of the perceived lack of information they received from the physician or the hospital staff. When the anger hit, the doctor was an easy place to focus.

I have been amazed at how many people get angry with clergy. Our expectations of clergy are often so high they cannot possibly measure up. Somehow we think ministers should perform some magic and make the pain go away. They preach how God will take care of us. Where is all that care?

The one dangerous place for anger to focus is internally. Anger has a way of turning inside and focusing on the grieving person. A great deal of the guilt we find in grief is not guilt, it is internalized anger. We begin to obsessively play the "if only" game. We build elaborate scenarios to prove it was somehow our fault. Nothing anyone can say seems to help. I am amazed at how often that happens. A nine-year-old girl whose father had been killed in a car wreck said, "I should have been with him; I should have been there." What could a nine-year-old little girl do to prevent a car wreck?

A woman whose daughter-in-law was murdered said, "I was there when my kids were looking for an apartment. I found that apartment. I took them over to see that apartment. If they had not been in that apartment the murderer would not have found her there, so it is all my fault."

When the anger has internalized, it is useless to argue or explain. The only thing that works is for someone to help us discover that we are dealing with anger. If we begin to see it, we can move beyond it.

A couple whose daughter had died of suicide asked to drive me to an airport ninety miles away. I thought we would deal with the death of their daughter. For the first hour of that ride they unloaded on all of their friends, their church and the pastor. I let them talk until the anger peaked and then asked if I could tell them what I had heard them say. When they agreed I said, "What I am hearing is that you are angry. It is all right to be angry. You should be angry." In the next thirty minutes their anger refocused. It was almost like an automatic focusing camera. When they realized they were angry, they began to talk about their feelings of anger instead of the external focus of that anger. I knew some of their friends and, through them, I was able to keep up with these people. Their anger never returned to its former focus. They now lead grief support groups in that area. When we arrived at the airport, the wife said, "You know why I have been so mad at those folks? I didn't want to be angry with my daughter."

Gradually we move through the reaction layer to. . .

Layer Four—Reconstruction.

We do not get well. We turn the corner in the way we cope. The pain that was so severe when our grief was young will not go away, but in time, it will become a dull ache. Usually we will know when we turn the corner. It will be a very evident event. Something we cannot do now we will suddenly be able to do. A chair we can't bring ourselves to sit in. Clothes we have not been able to remove from the closet. A room we left just as it was can now be changed.

One woman said she was walking to her car after church and suddenly she knew she had to decide right then whether or not to live again. She decided to live.

I told another woman that in her own way and on her own schedule she would decide to live again and there would be something to let her know. She said, "It is the desk in my den. It is a roll top desk and it contains all of the family pictures. I locked it. When I can open it and clean it out, I will know." Several months passed. One night she called and asked me to come. When I arrived she was standing by her desk and it was open and cleaned. She had decided to live again.

I met a little lady in Pasadena who had an automobile. She raised her hand to say, "You have just explained my husband's fifty-five Packard. He loved that car, and when he died I had to fight my whole family for the right to keep it. They thought seeing the car would remind me of my husband and be too painful. I won the fight. I can't tell you how much anger I worked off polishing that old Packard. It had more chrome on it than any car I ever saw. I would polish it and cuss Charlie for dying. One day I woke up and wanted to sell the car. I ran an ad and the first person who saw the car bought it. When he drove away, he had the same silly looking grin on his face that my husband had the day he bought it, and it was OK."

In brief, normal grief has periods of:
Shock and denial
Reality and hopelessness
Reaction and anger
Renewal and reconstruction.

That is normal for the grief following the death of a loved one. The grief during a long-term illness has some important differences we need to notice. The descriptions in this chapter lay the groundwork for us to understand the comparisons and differences.

Chapter VI

Slow Grief

If grief is like peeling an onion, the grief of long-term care is an onion sitting half peeled and smelling bad. This grief is never completed. Matter of fact, any progress in the grieving process is minimal at best. We seem to go just far enough to find the hurt and then our grief is put on hold with no elevator music in the background.

If there are four layers to the onion, during long-term care, we will be partially peeling all of them at once. There is no logical progression to this kind of grief. We will start the reality layer and the reaction layer while we are still in shock and disbelief. It is like starting four computer programs at the same time and never doing much with any of them. We start the programs and just leave them running on the screen. We might come by and click on one every once in a while but we are too busy to stop and work. We are so busy giving care and worrying about our loved one that we have no time to take care of our feelings as they arise. We know they are there, but we just ignore them and hope they will go away. Or we promise to deal with them some other time. The computer keeps running and the onion sits un-peeled.

The shock and disbelief can last for the whole length of the illness. A lady called last week to tell about her husband's fight with cancer. The type, location, and advanced state of his cancer meant he was not going to live very long no matter what kind of treatments were applied.

She said, "When he died I was totally shocked. When I tell my friends how shocked I was they look at me like I am crazy or stupid, but it never one time dawned upon me that he could die. Then he was gone. Right when I thought we were winning, he was gone. I am having a horrible time with my grief. I can't make my friends and family understand the shock I feel. He was not going to die."

My neighbor lost his wife to cancer. During the long battle his medical team and friends would suggest hospice care, but they would not even consider such a thing. Hospice was for people who were dying. She was not dying. I visited her the day before she died. Anyone could see she would not make it more than a few hours. Anyone except her husband. He was shocked beyond belief when she died.

We do not move very far beyond the shock and disbelief. Everyone else will see your loved one's condition long before you do. You are not blind nor stupid, you are just in that period of shock and denial and cannot seem to move on.

Reality only comes late in the night when we cannot drive it back down into the recesses of our brain. It rears its ugly head and we have brief glimpses of our accumulating losses. We realize how lonely we are, how tired we are, how much we miss affection and companionship. We long for communication about something other than the illness. We shed a few tears and have a brief time of feeling sorry for ourselves, but soon the guilt takes over and we begin to tell ourselves how selfish we are. How can we feel sorry for ourselves when our loved one is in such a horrible condition?

The preacher use to say, "I felt sorry that I had no shoes until I met a man who had no feet." That sounds good, but it doesn't work. In the middle of winter, I still want shoes even if no one has feet. Our own needs don't go away, just because someone has greater needs. Our pain does not fade away at the sight of someone else with greater pain.

The anger rises to chest level and sits there building toward some terrible explosion we do not think we can allow to happen. It comes out in irritability about small things. It comes out in depression. It comes out in illness. It focuses on us and makes us feel guilty and responsible. But it is never welcomed to the surface. It is never explored and expressed openly. How can I possibly be angry? I am not the one who is sick.

Repressed Emotions

Unfortunately grief is not the only emotion frozen on hold. Caregivers may also be repressing emotions of:

Family Pressures

Many caregivers are also facing tremendous pressure from family members. Many are not only providing care, but are also receiving criticisms and second–guessing from the rest of the family. You may have been assigned the caregiving task by family members who do not help and yet feel free to criticize. If a family is ever going to divide, it will do so over the care of aging loved ones.

The tendency is to delay the dealing with these pressures and criticisms. It is easy to convince ourselves that this is not the time to bring these things up. It might be upsetting to the loved one. It might cause problems within the family. We tell ourselves we will take care of it after this is all over. In the meantime we may be living in a pressure cooker of repressed emotions.

Anger Toward The Situation

You have lost your life. Most of the things you enjoyed are gone. There is no longer time for many of the things that enhanced your life.

Life is an hour by hour, day by day test of survival. You live from one doctor's appointment to the next treatment. If you are giving care from a distance then you live from one phone call to the next. You cannot make plans nor live your life because you "never know what might happen." Every phone call brings a bolt of fear into your heart and the tension never lessens. This must create a sorrow that will not go away. There must be regrets, anger, even self pity somewhere inside of you. And this, too, must go on hold.

Guilt

The guilt also adds to the load. A woman said, "I never thought my father would be a burden to me. I was totally unprepared for that feeling. How could I dare feel burdened? He gave so much to my life, and now I feel burdened because I must care for him?"

I said, "Did you ever stop to think of how many times your father felt like you were a burden? When you were young and not responding to his parenting, don't you know he thought how much easier it would have been if he did not have so many mouths to feed?"

She laughed and said, "I have felt that way about my children at times, but I never thought my father might have felt that way about me. It is just my turn to feel burdened isn't it?"

Insecurities

Caregiving is a process of making a whole lot of medical decisions with very little knowledge or expertise. When family or friends disagree with the decisions, the insecurities can be almost overwhelming. "Why is the doctor doing that?", can give one a case of the internal hives. None of us feel as though we know what we are doing in this area. Therefore, the pressure mounts.

The Valley Is Lonesome

Caring for a loved one is hard work. I can think of none harder. The pressure we feel is unrelenting. The hours are never-ending. Just the physical endurance required in giving care is exhausting.

If the physical side was all we had to handle we could do it. We would be tired, but we could manage. The emotional side causes the exhaustion.

The feelings we may not, or cannot, express–the anger, the frustration, the regrets–all of these add to our burden.

When all of these are stacked on our shoulders we suddenly discover the physical is the easy part. The emotional is the killer.

Chapter VII

Two Healing Words

The question is, what can we do about all of these feelings? How do we respond when we have no emotions to spare? When our whole existence is dominated with giving care. When it is not possible to complete the grieving. What do we do then? May I introduce you to a couple of very healing concepts?

Significance

When bad things happen to us, the first thing we want to do, and the first thing we need to do, is establish the significance of that event. My grandson came to me in tears saying his cousin had hit him. The normal parenting response would be to say, "You are being a tattle tale and a crybaby. Now go back in there and you kids play nice or I will have to come in there and separate you." That day I knelt beside him and said, "I am sorry that happened to you." His face lit up and he said, "You want to go play catch?" All he needed was the right to establish the significance of what happened to him. Once that was accomplished he could move on to better things.

That is human nature. Anyone who has had surgery knows this need. The first thing we

want to do is show the scar. If we can't do that,
we will talk about the surgery as long as anyone
will act like they are still listening. We will tell
how bad our case was, all of the bad things we
experienced during the whole hospital stay, and
how serious and unusual our surgery was. "I
didn't just have surgery I had the worst surgery
that ever was! My gall bladder weighed forty-six
pounds, it took a doctor and two nurses to lift
it, and it is a miracle that I am alive." That is
called establishing the significance of an event.

When my wife had heart by-pass surgery we
were in the hospital for an extended period of
time. Every time one of the family returned to
the sitting area after going somewhere in the
hospital, the group would immediately ask what
stories they had heard. In any hospital in the
world, total strangers will tell you what they are
going through. Hospitals are full of folks who
are desperate to establish the significance of
what is happening to them and no one seems to
have time to hear.

The remarkable thing is that once we have
established significance we can move on. My
grandson was ready to play ball as soon as
someone heard his story. If we cannot find a
way to establish significance we do not move on.
We stay there and try again and again to find
some way to be heard. If the hurt is deep
enough, and our efforts are futile over a long

period of time, then the event becomes an obsession to us.

I have finished a book on long-term hurts and grudges. A grudge does not happen because someone is too hard headed to forgive. A grudge happens when someone is hurt and they never get the chance to establish the significance of that hurt. When they try, they are not heard. Not being heard adds rejection and disinterest to the pain. Over time a grudge develops and dominates a life. We hear how we should "forgive and forget". We hear how "we should put it all behind us and get on with our lives". Both of these sound good, but they cannot be done until we have established the significance of what has happened to us.

Self Discovery

This is why I asked you to make a list of your losses. The first step in establishing significance is the self discovery of what you are experiencing. Most of the time caregivers are so involved in the care that they never stop and analyze what they are losing in the process. We hurt with undefined pain. Most of that is caused by the lack of time, but some of it is caused by being afraid to look. We don't want to feel sorry for ourselves so we try not to think about it. We put it on the back burner and promise to think about it tomorrow. We are afraid that dredging it up will leave us depressed, or that we will start feeling sorry for ourselves. No one wants to become some old whining bore that no one wants to be around, and we are afraid that thinking about our situation will lead to being just that kind of bore.

We need to establish the significance of these losses because they are the ones that hurt us. When we are hurt we are also angry, although we may not realize the anger is there. Swallowed, or internalized, anger leads to depression. Our choice is to face it and make the effort of trying to establish significance, or internalize all of these feelings and let them eat away at us from the inside. Even if facing them makes us sad for a while—even if facing them makes us feel like we are whining babies—it is still better to face and establish the significance of the loss than it is to hide and swallow a hurt that keeps gnawing at our insides.

Permission

The second step is to give yourself permission to have whatever feelings you need. The best advice I can offer to anyone in grief is to feel what you feel. You cannot change those feelings, so the options are to fight what you feel or to relax and let them just happen. Accept them as normal. The more you fight them, the more intense they become. You begin to be healthy when you can say, "I am mad about this and I have a right to be mad. I should be angry. Who wouldn't be angry if this happened to them?" When you can say that, you are giving yourself the gift of significance.

Journal

In addition to the list you might find other ways to get the feelings out for a look. Some people keep a journal. A journal has many other uses as well. It helps to keep the dates of when the doctor started certain medications or treatments. It helps to keep a journal of what your loved one says during this illness. Often there are funny experiences along the way that will become very precious memories later on. Your record of these times will become a treasure. It also helps to keep a record of how you felt. What you were experiencing could help you encourage others in the future. A journal is also a good way to keep your feelings on the surface and visible where they can be acknowledged.

Expression

In an earlier chapter I referred to keeping your "cussing current". I am not necessarily recommending the use of foul language. You need to use the language you are comfortable with, and you should use the strongest language you are comfortable with. Sometimes the English language is just not adequate. So with whatever language you want to use, keep your cussing current. It is all right to gripe about your situation. I don't think it is neither kind nor appropriate to gripe to the one to whom you are giving care. But you need to find some place to gripe—some place to express how you feel—and let'er rip.

We need to establish significance inside ourselves, but the real establishing of significance requires someone who will listen to us. If the first healing word is "significance," then the second one is "understanding."

Understanding

The longer I live, the more I love the word understanding. When we get to the bottom line, most of us just want to be understood. It feels wonderful to have our feelings given credence and to have our thoughts legitimized. Everyone wants to be understood.

If a woman comes into my office and says, "I don't know what is wrong, but I don't love my husband anymore. I am not angry at him, he has not done anything to make me feel this way, and I have no reason to feel this way. But, I suddenly realized that I have very little feelings for him anymore."

If we trace those feelings back it is amazing
how often we find a woman who has never been
understood. Every time she had a thought she
was told either in words, tone of voice, attitudes,
or body language that she was wrong to think
that way. Every time she verbalized her feelings
she was made to feel stupid for feeling the way
she felt. Every time that happens to us, we feel
unfulfilled and diminished. That diminishing
does not go away, it builds up until one day it
shuts off feelings toward the unresponsive
person.

All of us have deep feelings that we need to
have understood. Caregiving creates a world of
these feelings that long for an understanding
ear. Wouldn't it be great to have some place
where we could pour it all out and no one would
argue or explain away or criticize how we feel?

Some of us can't find the words to express
our feelings. We are caught between words.
A woman in Canada said:

*"I did not know what happened to
me until I heard you explain about being
understood. My son died. There was a
party, the group was drinking, and there
was a gun there. The gun went off and my
son died. I had a horrible time with the
word 'accident'. An 'accident' is when cars
wreck or lightening strikes. If a guy has a*

gun in his hand with his finger on the trigger, and the gun goes off, that is more than an accident. Every time I would say that, someone would ask if I thought he was murdered. I would say no, but it was more than an 'accident'."

"I finally went to see one of my son's friends who was there the night he died. When I arrived, the friend was very tense. He was a paraplegic and was sitting in his wheel chair with his hands up in a defensive position. I said, 'John, I am having a terrible time with the word accident'."

"He dropped his hands and sighed, 'So am I.' I began to get well that day." Someone understood.

As with significance, if we can be understood we can move on. If no one understands, we gradually build an obsession.

I met two sisters who said their mother remembered every hurt she had ever experienced and was a totally negative person. I asked them what their mother said to them most often.

They responded, "The thing she says that hurts us the most is, 'My life stopped the day my little boy died.' She still has us and our brother died sixty-one years ago."

I said, " The next time she says that, touch her and say, 'Mom, how did that make you feel?'"

Most likely, when her son died, she never found anyone who would listen or understand how she felt, so sixty-one years later she is still trying.

The opposite of understanding is not misunderstanding—it is trivialization. We trivialize the pain people feel when we try to explain it away or put the best face on what happened to them. When it happens to us we feel as if our pain does not matter, or that we are exaggerating and making mountains out of mole hills because we think our pain is worth mentioning. And it also makes us angry.

Telling someone whose child has just died that God will not put more on them than they can bear is maddening instead of comforting. Trying to tell someone how much worse the situation could be or how lucky they are that the illness is not worse, diminishes them and does not relieve their pain.

I had cancer surgery a few years ago. I grew so tired of being trivialized that I stopped telling anyone about the fact that I was to have the surgery. Folks would quote some clichè and dismiss the surgery from the conversation. I even had someone say, "Aren't you glad you have the GOOD cancer?" Calling any cancer good is an oxymoron if there ever was one. I wanted to tell someone, and I had already worn out my wife's ears, so I called a friend whom I had known since childhood. When I said, "I have cancer," she said an expletive and then began to cry. After a few moments she stopped and said, "Oh Doug! I should not have said that word to you and I ought not to be crying. I should be trying to cheer you up." I said, "Hush! You are messing up the only appropriate response I have had so far." That is how I felt and it was wonderful having someone else who felt the same way I did. I was understood and I felt better.

When understanding is combined with significance a healing force is applied to our hurts. It is hard to believe these two words will work. They seem to be just the opposite of what we have always been taught about helping others find healing. Letting people talk and cry about their pain has not been considered the normal approach. Explaining how they should feel and then telling them to buck up and get over it is more the American way of facing hurt.

We have been programmed to believe:

Sympathy Makes It Worse

I was raised to believe we should never sympathize with people. Sympathy is like pouring gasoline on a fire. I was taught that people feed on the sympathy and never get any better. Now, here I am, saying sympathy is the first response needed if we are to help people.

Our fear of sympathy forces us to turn a cold shoulder to the pain a loved one feels. At a recent conference a man told about his father having to sell his farm in Indiana and move to Pennsylvania to live in his son's house. The father was born on that farm and so was his father before him. To be forced into selling a farm that had been in the family for so long had to have been a painful experience.

The man said, "My father keeps trying to talk about the farm, and I am afraid if he talks about it he will just miss it more and it will make the move more painful. When he brings it up, I immediately change the subject. I have not let him talk about it at all. Now I am hearing you say that I should let him talk. That, as he talks, he will establish the significance of his loss and will have received the gift of understanding from me."

That is exactly what I had been saying. When that father gets through establishing significance he will be able to move on. If he is not allowed to do so, he will be trying to talk about the farm till the day he dies. All he needs is for the son to hear him and then say, "I am very sorry this has happened to you."

We Think Tears Are Corrosive

Nothing seems to create more discomfort than seeing someone else cry. Even the most caring people react by trying to stop tears as quickly as possible. Most of us are uncomfortable in that kind of intimacy. We seem to be afraid the situation will get out of control and we will not know how to get it back in order. It is hard to sit and hold someone's hand while they cry, but that is just the thing hurting people need someone to do. We do not have to do anything more than that.

When someone hurts they need The Three "H's" They need someone to HANG AROUND, HUG THEM AND HUSH. We don't have to say anything. We don't have to have answers. We don't have to fix anything. All they need is for us to be there, hug them, if that is appropriate, and let them talk until they are finished.

We Think Stoicism Is Strength

I wish Jackie Kennedy had cried in public when President Kennedy was shot. We have that memory of her standing on the steps of the Capitol in quiet control while John Jr. saluted his father. The whole world seem to say, "What dignity! What strength! What grace!" Contrast that with England when Princess Diana died. They almost demanded that the Queen cry and they stacked London knee deep in flowers as they openly mourned their princess. Guess which one is the most healthy.

We Think We Can Change The Way People Feel By Changing The Way They Think

We have always believed that if we can just give people a new way of thinking about what they are experiencing they will feel much better. This leads to an awful lot of hurtful explanations about why there is suffering, and very little that helps them with their feelings. Feelings do not always follow thought. How many times have you heard someone say, "I know that is right, but that is not how I feel about it." If feelings are going to change, someone must accept those feelings, try to understand the pain, and resist the urge to try to change how the person feels. That is another way of saying we need the gifts of understanding and significance.

So what does that all mean to someone who is spending every day consumed with the needs of a loved one with a debilitating disease? It means you have the right to complain about what you are going through. To do so is not being selfish nor is it the whining of a child. Matter of fact, it is nature's way of helping us cope with bad situations. Significance will not make it all better. Significance will not change the circumstances. Significance will simply make the circumstances more bearable.

This book is aimed at the caregiver but, while the subject is fresh, it needs to be said that the patient also needs these same two magical words. They need the right to establish the significance of what they are losing. Sympathy will not make them worse. "Putting the best face on it" also trivializes what they are feeling. They, too, need someone to simply say they are sorry and give the gift of understanding.

Chapter VIII

Share My Lonesome Valley

There is an old joke that concludes, "When you are up to your ears in alligators, it is hard to remember that your primary purpose was to drain the swamp." When we are way over our ears in giving care, who has the time to worry about taking care of ourselves or of working through our grief? This is grief on the run. This must be grief in little spurts at odd times. We cannot complete the process because we keep suffering more and more losses all the time.

So the question becomes, "How can we find a way to be healthy in the middle of the sickness? How can we be understood and establish significance on the run?"

The Value Of Groups

Almost every city, and most small towns, have access to small group meetings designed to give care to caregivers. Almost every disease has special groups that meet to give help to each other in dealing with that particular disease. There are Alzheimer's Associations in many cities who serve those folks who are dealing with Alzheimer's and other forms of dementia. These are wonderful organizations.

They are the best source for information about these diseases. Good information is hard to find and very helpful when found. This organization also provides support groups for those giving care. I cannot recommend these groups enough. They are a must.

It is unfortunate that people are so reluctant to admit that their loved one has a disease like Alzheimer's. Somehow we connect this disease with losing our minds and the shame of it can drive us into denial or make us reluctant to participate in groups for fear someone will know. Alzheimer's Disease and other forms of dementia are real diseases. They are not some emotional breakdown or some failure in the character of the person. They are not diseases that happen to those with weak minds. Some of the smartest and most dynamic people who have ever lived have developed Alzheimer's Disease. This is something to be faced openly and without apology. If we can do so, there is help available.

Going to a group meeting sounds strange and even a little scary, but nothing else that I know of can give more comfort and help. Finding out that others are facing the same kind of things you face helps. There is great relief in discovering that they are not coping with the disease any better than you are. To learn that you are not the only one who gets frustrated or angry at the patient can relieve a great deal of the guilt you feel. Discovering you aren't the only one who feels burdened by the care giving can make you feel normal.

There are agencies for many other illnesses such as Parkinson's, cancer, stroke, heart disease, and AIDS. These are equally effective and helpful. Caregiving to one disease can be very much like any other disease, but it just helps to talk to other people who are dealing with a similair situation.

These support groups are listed in the phone book. There is a short list at the back of this book. Every county has access to an Area Agency On Aging. They are also listed in the phone book. This agency has information about every help available to aging people and publishes a guide for each county or area. They have Ombudsmen available to help families who have a problem with care agencies. This is a wonderfully valuable source that is ready to help.

In many cities there are centers that provide adult day care. I have toured many of these facilities around the country. Some are built and funded by communities, others by churches or other organizations. I find it ironic that almost every one of the facilities I have visited report that the number one problem is getting families to use the service. Too many people think they are some how failing to care if they don't provide every minute of the care themselves. They feel guilty for taking a loved one to day care. They are afraid of being criticized by family or friends. The loved one may have a wonderful time of socialization in the process, but the caregiver can't stand to let someone else give the care, so many facilities operate at far less than capacity.

Many cities have Meals On Wheels programs for those who find it hard to prepare meals at home. Many cities now have grocery stores that will deliver food and many restaurants are developing home delivery services. If finances permit, it helps to find someone to clean the house on occasion. Dropping off the clothes at a full service laundry can also be a wonderful relief. Help is available if you can give yourself permission to take advantage and allow others to provide some of the care.

The Value Of Friends

Agencies and groups can help, but it takes friends who listen to make us feel understood and to help us establish the significance of our loss. Finding these friends may be difficult. Almost everyone who suffers the death of a loved one will also lose friends. The loss of friends is the loss most mentioned in the grief conferences I conduct. The friends don't know what to say and they feel awkward in the presence of so much intense pain. They find it hard to return and so they delay until they feel so guilty about not being there they can't go back. Gradually they drop away.

People in long-term care also lose friends. The friends don't know what to say in these situations either and they feel the same awkwardness and dread the visits. They can also seem to be rather shallow and silly to those who are in the pain. When a friend's husband was dying, a woman who came by to visit began talking about her company changing computer software and that she had lost her old e-mail address. She became so worked up over this that she cried. My friend said, "I wanted to shake her and say, 'All of this over an e-mail address? Get a life!'"

Unfortunately, there are not very many people who know how to just listen and understand. Most of the time most people will follow a set pattern of responses. When someone expresses some problem or pain the natural responses are:

Explanation

The first response is to explain why this happened or how it could have been worse.

People feel compelled to try to "Put the best face on it" and thus make you feel better. Most folks really think they can change the way you feel by changing the way you think, so they will conjure up several explanations. Get ready for some rather terrible, and often harsh, reasons for your pain.

I had a friend whose child was killed in a car wreck. Someone told him, "Perhaps your little girl would have grown up to be a bad person and God took her home before she could do so." How comforting could that be? The person who said that was not a bad person. The person who said that was trying to help. The problem was that person thought help meant giving some kind of explanation that defended God, but did nothing to deal with, or understand, the pain of that grieving father.

Argument

If explanations don't work some people will try to argue with you:
Now you cannot let yourself feel this way.
You must put this all behind you and move on.
There is no reason for you to feel guilty, so stop feeling that way.

You will hear several statements like these during your walk through the valley. These friends are trying to help, but they think they can change the way you feel by changing the way you think.

Criticism

If explanations and argument fail, get ready for the big guns:

You are not trying to get over this.
You could deal with your guilt if you
just wanted to do so.
You are setting yourself up for martyrdom.

It is just a natural progression. When people find someone in pain they try to explain it away. When explanations do not work, they argue. If the person is too hard-headed to heed this great advice, then they criticize, all in the name of helping you with your pain or grief.

Build Your Own Support System

You do not have the time nor the energy to go through this pattern. You do not need to be subjected to any of it and it will not help. You can, however, build your own support group. Choose a friend or two and ask them to read these last two chapters. Then sit down and tell them what you need. Most people want to help if they can, but they just don't know what to say or when to say it. If they are clearly told that all you need is someone to hang around, hug them, and hush, it can help them become comfortable doing just that. They will not feel as though

they have to say something in order to help. The
use these friends as long as their ears hold out.
They can give you the gifts of understanding and
significance. I know of no greater help than thos
two gifts.

Chapter IX

Defend Yourself

Now is the time for all of the primary caregivers to rise up and defend themselves. Some will find it harder to do than others. Some accepted the task because the loved one is a spouse or partner and you have been taking care of each other for many years. Giving care is as natural as breathing. The thought of asking anyone to help would be a sacrilege. Others became caregivers because of geographic location or because the rest of the family was not in a position to give the care. Some accepted in the hope of attaining the love they have worked for all of their lives. If you are the caregiver for any of these reasons, you will find it very hard to ask for help and have an even harder time accepting any help offered.

No matter the reason, the very fact that you accepted the task means you are the type of person who will find it hard to defend your needs. You will give and give without complaint. In the process of caring you may do harm to yourself. For that reason I have prepared what I call the "Primary Caregiver's Bill Of Rights." I hope you will post one copy on your bathroom mirror and give another copy to all family members.

The Primary Caregiver's
Bill of Rights

◆

The right to rest

The right to honesty

The right to not be second—guessed
about medical decisions

The right to family sensitivity
about time and expense

The right to receive thanks

𝒯𝒽𝑒 𝒫𝓇𝒾𝓂𝒶𝓇𝓎 𝒞𝒶𝓇𝑒𝑔𝒾𝓋𝑒𝓇𝓈
𝓑𝒾𝓁𝓁 𝒪𝒻 𝓡𝒾𝑔𝒽𝓉𝓈

The Right To Rest

Caregiving is grueling work. I watched a neighbor try to be full-time nurse to her mother who was in a coma. I decided no one has been created yet who is strong enough to be a full-time nurse over an extended period of time. The physical part is hard enough, but when the emotional grind is added, it becomes more than one human being can endure without periods of escape and rest.

The other family members need to be sure the caregiver has these times for rest. The caregiver will have hundreds of excuses such as, "The time is not right. The loved one is not doing well right now, so maybe I can take off at a later date. It seems like every time I leave there is a turn for the worse." The family may have to bodily remove the caregiver, but there must be times of rest.

The Right To Honesty

The family must agree to one basic rule. If they do not like the care that is being given by the primary caregiver, they will talk to the caregiver in person. They should not discuss it with other family members before they talk to the primary caregiver. They will go directly to the caregiver. After having this discussion, the family member will then either drop the issue and agree with the caregiver or that family member will take over that part of the job which is being questioned.

If a family is ever going to split up, they most likely will do so over the care of a loved one. The only way to avoid misunderstanding is to have an understanding. Face-to-face is the only way to have an understanding.

The physical part of the care is not what gets the caregiver down. It is the guilt and emotional upheavals heaped on by a disapproving family that makes the job unbearable.

The Right Not To Be Second Guessed About Medical Decisions.

Caring for an elderly or critically-ill loved one involves making a whole lot of medical decisions with very little information. I have no idea why physicians are so reluctant to talk to families of their patients. I have no idea why they think knowing the truth is such a bad thing. All I know is that decision-making in a time like this is blind guess work.

Then, the family comes for a visit and the second guessing starts. "Why are they doing this treatment?" "Why are you using THAT doctor?" "Why aren't you taking Mom to Mayo's?"

These may be legitimate questions, but they leave the caregiver in a state of panic and confusion. If a family member wants to be involved in the medical decisions, they should make any arrangements necessary to be there when those decisions are being made. If not, they should hush.

The Right To Family Sensitivity About Time And Expense

If a loved one is hospitalized or, if they become a resident of a nursing home, the primary caregiver's home becomes a bed and breakfast. Usually the primary caregiver lives near the loved one and their house may be the only one available. Therefore, when other members of the family come to visit, they stay with the caregiver.

We had company every weekend during the time we cared for my wife's mother. We enjoyed the company and they were helpful to us, but I could see that in some cases this could put a burden on the finances of the caregiver. Feeding people costs money. My own concern involved the lost time. It is hard to continue regular working routines with visitors in the home.

The family should recognize the cost and the time and be as self-sufficient as possible. They shouldn't expect food service and entertainment.

The Right To Receive Thanks

After we gave care to my mother-in-law, my wife's sister and brother insisted we go on a trip paid for out of the inheritance. The trip was wonderful, but the expression of thanks was even better. Having our work acknowledged is another way of saying they helped us establish the significance of our care giving.

I have heard too many stories of caregivers who gave care while the family criticized and made them feel guilty, and when the help was over, no one ever said a word of thanks. A simple "thank you" will go a long way toward helping the caregiver rest up from the ordeal.

Section III

Facing The Future

Friends are the dearest
When the valley is deepest.

Chapter X

End-Of-Life Decisions

The day came when I had to decide whether to continue forcing nourishment to my father. We had already made the hard transition from medical care to palliative care. Palliative care meant they stopped trying to cure my father and started trying to make the rest of his time as comfortable as possible. This is usually when hospice enters the picture.

There was no hospice in our town when my father died. I have gone through the loss of both my father and a brother who needed hospice care and, in both cases, it was not available. After two such deaths, I am an absolute fanatic in my support of this great program. When the time comes to make this transition, these people are wonderfully supportive and, believe me, support is important.

Now we faced the second difficult transition. The physician asked if we wished to continue nourishment for my father. We were fortunate to have a physician who would ask the question. Far too often physicians cannot think in these terms. They are trained and committed to fight for life as long as possible and doing anything less than that is unthinkable to them. Recent

advances in modern medicine create a conflict
for both the physician and the family. With
modern technology we can prolong life far
beyond the possibility of having any quality, and
yet, no one wants to make the decision to stop
trying. This is the decision I was facing and the
decision that some of you who are reading this
book will have to face.

How do you decide to starve a loved one?
Does that not mean you are condemning them
to a slow and agonizing death? Those are the
questions raised by the media in a recent case
in Virginia when a wife decided to stop
nourishment for her husband who had been in
a vegetative state for several years following an
auto accident. The governor intervened and it
became a media circus. The media kept saying
his wife was "condemning him to a slow
agonizing death". They made these statements
in spite of physicians' interviews that revealed
just the opposite to be true. These experiences
make this decision all the harder and the guilt
all the deeper.

I had the good fortune of having two things to
support me in my decision. First, I had met a
very honest physician at one of my seminars.
He specialized in geriatric medicine and worked
exclusively in nursing homes. He started our
conversation by saying:

*"I have stopped going to the wealthy
nursing homes. Rich people think they can
buy anything, so they pressured me to do
things to their elderly loved ones that sent
me home in tears every night. There comes
a time when the body shuts down.
There is no sense running a blood test, the
person is not making any blood. You know
the count is low without testing. There is
no point in running urine samples, you
already know the results. There is no
sense giving them shots, they don't have
enough muscle to absorb the medicine and
it does more harm than good. I couldn't
take that any more."*

I asked him about nourishment. He said,
"Unless the heart stops, that is how everyone dies.
The body loses the ability to absorb food and death
comes from lack of nourishment. You can put the
food in there but you are doing so to make
yourself feel better. It does nothing for the
patient."

I asked if this was a slow, painful death. He
said, "To the contrary. Over a few days time the
person will slip into a coma and death will not be
prolonged nor painful."

My second source of support and assurance
was the fact that I knew what my father wanted,
and I knew where the rest of the family stood on
this issue. I knew because we had talked about it.

I am not writing this chapter to recommend that families stop nourishing dying loved ones. I am writing this chapter to encourage families to know where they stand and to know as far in advance as possible. I urge families to have a family meeting to discuss the issues of long-term care, and to have that meeting as far ahead of need as possible. I am sixty-seven years old and in good health. That is an ideal time for my family to begin the discussion of how we will face the future. If there is a serious diagnosis made, the family should begin talking as soon as possible.

Even though the families reading this book are already deeply involved in care after a discouraging diagnosis, many will not have discussed the issues at all. It is very hard to discuss these kinds of things. It is harder still to discuss these kinds of things with family. Most of us are afraid to have intimate conversations with family members. There is too much at stake and we are afraid of conflict. Every time I mention family meeting in my conferences the audience seems to freeze and starts saying, "My family would never do such a thing".

The need for discussion adds another duty to the already loaded world of the primary caregiver. Most likely he or she must be the person who calls the meeting and insist on each family member being present.

When the meeting starts, the primary caregiver should be sure everyone else talks first. No one should be a spectator. Spectators become critics. The primary caregiver should simply get their attention and then say, "None of us want to talk about such things, but in the future we are going to be forced into some decisions we never thought we would have to make. It is important that each of our views are heard and that we come to some kind of consensus on several areas."

Some of the areas I can think of are:

"What if our loved one needs more care than we can provide in the home?"

How will that decision be made? What kind of care will the family be comfortable with? What are the deciding factors as to when that decision will be made? Do we wait for the physician to make the call? Do we set our own parameters?

"If our loved one requires special care in the home, or if a nursing home becomes necessary, how will we deal with the financial expenses of such care?"

Who will administrate the funds? Will it be necessary for the family to participate? If so, how will that be done in an equitable manner?

"What if our loved one needs medical decisions made and is no longer able to make those decisions. How are we equipped now?"

What do we need to become equipped? Who should be designated to make these choices? Do we have a Living Will signed? Do we have a Durable Power Of Attorney For Health Care signed? If not, how can we get these documents prepared and signed?

"How do you think you will feel if, in spite of our Living Will and Durable Power Of Attorney, we must make a decision to stop nourishing our loved one?"

If the loved one is able to give an opinion on this matter, it certainly should be heard by the whole group. If the loved one has expressed an opinion on this matter in the past, it should be discussed in the group. The night before the decision needs to be made is much too late for someone to tell the rest of the family what they think the loved one would want. This needs to be made clear as early as possible and with as much discussion as possible.

This is also a good time to discuss the funeral arrangements. Every funeral home offers programs to pre-plan a funeral. This might be the best time to take care of many of the details. If Medicaid is going to be needed to finance long-term care of an elderly loved one, there may be a need to reduce the estate down to Medicaid standards. The law allows a person to pre-pay the funeral cost and it not count against the total value of the estate.

Long—Term Care Decisions

If your loved one has Alzheimer's, Parkinson's, or other debilitating diseases, the chances are good that a nursing home will be needed. It is wise for the family to begin investigating the availability of these facilities. Nursing homes have changed radically in the last few years. They now offer many levels of care and it is important to match the level of care with the level of need. It is not a good idea to place a loved one in a facility that gives more care than they need. That is expensive and the loved one will not be happy. Likewise, it is not appropriate to chose a facility that furnishes less care than needed.

Some of the levels of care now offered to people in need of long-term care include:

Retirement Living

These facilities offer a wide range of living options but do not provide any nursing care or physical assistance.

Assisted Living

Assisted living is just what the title suggests. These facilities offer the assistance a person needs to function on their own. Assisted living does not offer nursing care, although some make this care available through home health agencies. Some areas even have assisted living centers for Alzheimer's patients in the early stages.

Nursing Facilities

These are called by several names such as acute care, nursing home, or health care center. These offer full-time nursing to patients who need medication and on-going intense care.

It would be helpful if the family would tour some of these facilities to understand the care levels. When the decisions need to be made, those family members who live away will have a vision of what kind of care is being chosen.

While the family is touring the facilities, they should check out which ones offer respite care. Respite care means your loved one can go to the facility for a week or so at a time while the caregiver takes some time off. One of the nicest things a family can do for the primary caregiver is to find this care and insist the caregiver take advantage of the opportunity. As we mentioned in an earlier chapter, the same thing that makes a person a caregiver also makes them resist rest. The family must intervene and insist. If the family finds the respite care and insists on the caregiver using the service, it may relieve some of the guilt from the decision.

Once again I must say it: *The only way to avoid misunderstanding is to have an understanding.* Long-term care decisions need the discussions that lead to understanding and agreement.

If nursing home care becomes a necessity, one more sorrow and a great deal of guilt is added to the burden of the caregiver. I promised my parents and my wife's parents they would never live in a nursing home. My wife's mother died in a nursing home. My father died in a nursing home. My mother died in an assisted-living center. In spite of my promises, and, in spite of it being one of the hardest decisions of my life, it became necessary for them to receive this kind of care.

One of the prices we pay for modern medical care is we may live beyond our family's ability to care for us. I promised my father he would never go, and I kept the promise. He just outlived the promise. He needed more care than I could provide and the day came when we had to make the decision. It hurt and I felt guilty to the core of my being. All I could say was that I gave all the care I was able to give, and he lived beyond my ability to provide for his needs.

Hospice And Home Health Care

While the family is investigating their options, is a good time to explore the hospice and home health care availability in the community. Some communities will have several home health agencies and hospices. Discovering the care these agencies offer can provide a great deal of help and peace of mind.

Hospice care is available if the physician determines that a patient has six months or less to live. A family has the right to make a request for hospice care and should not be timid or reticent in doing so. Hospice provides wonderful, caring nurses trained in comfort and pain management, chaplains, social workers, and bereavement specialists. Too often families delay in making the decision to use hospice because they think this is a decision to die. It is a decision to live, as fully as possible, for as long as possible, in as little pain as possible. Hospice eases the loved one's pain, and the burden for the family.

Chapter XI

Walking Through The Valley

After my neighbor's wife died of cancer, he would not go to any support groups and told me he was not comfortable talking about her death. He did read my grief books and then made excuses to just catch me in the yard. We did grief counseling over the lawn mower. He would mention in every session that his wife had not used hospice. He would say, "We thought hospice was for dying people and she wasn't going to die. When she died, I was the most shocked person in the world. We never thought about her dying. We never talked about it at all." His voice would trail off and he would mumble, "There was so much we never did get to say."

We humans generally don't do death very well. We are afraid to even use the word. We talk about folks "passing" or being "lost." We seem to think if we ignore it, death will not happen. We think if a person ever admits they are dying they will give up and death will happen. If we can hide death from them they will live much longer.

There is no reason to hide the true condition from our loved ones. There is no reason to wonder if they should be told. If they are dying, they already know it. There is no way to keep it from them. There are too many clues. They overhear too many conversations in the hallways. They read it on the faces of their loved ones, and their bodies are telling them the truth about their condition. They know, and the family knows, but too often we find ourselves locked in "The Prison Of The Positive." We must be positive and keep up a good front, so our loved one will think all is well and then they won't give up hope and die. The loved one also must keep up a good front, because they sense that no one wants to talk about their true condition. So we visit in unreality and talk about unrelated things that do not matter, to keep from talking about the one thing that is dominating everyone's thoughts and is screaming to be heard. It is like the old story of an elephant in the room that no one would mention for fear no one else saw it.

This robs us of dying ritual. My grandfather died long before I was born. Something bit him and he developed blood poisoning. In those days that was a death sentence. He knew he was dying. His family knew he was dying. No one denied the fact. They talked about it in open conversation. He had the chance to call each of his children to his bedside for a time of talking and saying good-byes. When death approached, the whole family was around his bed helping him on his journey. That is dying ritual.

Now we isolate people and insulate them from the truth. Even though they know the real truth, we act as though they do not realize what is happening to them. We make happy noises and talk nonsense while their whole being screams out for a chance to talk about the experience of dying. People know they are dying and they usually want to talk about it. They will choose the people they wish to talk with if they are given the chance.

A woman asked to speak with me on several occasions. Each time the family would send for me, and then they would not leave the room so the lady could talk. They just could not let the talk happen. They thought that if she talked she would go ahead and die, so they would stand there by the bed while the woman and I stammered on about nothing.

One day in the hospital, while her husband was talking to someone on the other side of the room, she drew me close and said, "I am just so tired." I said, "Are you saying you want to go on?" She would not respond to that but said, "Well, I have those grandchildren." It had been necessary for her to raise her grandchildren. I told her she had done a good job and that they would be fine. Then I said, "If you are ready, it is all right to go on." She pulled me close and kissed me and, in two hours, she was gone. She just needed permission.

My Uncle Joe died about a month ago. Joe was only eight years older than I and we have been close all of our lives. After he took early retirement, he drove me to many speaking engagements and we had many wonderful experiences together. Joe had a heart attack and the time came when the doctors called the family together to say there was nothing more they could do. His heart was beating only because of a drip and his kidneys had completely shut down. Since Joe and I had talked so often about dying ritual and he had, in turn, told his family about his wishes, they asked the doctor to tell him. The doctor promised, but did not do so. I arrived the next day, which was Saturday, to find a family in panic. The doctor had left town for the week-end and Joe did not know about his condition. They were afraid he would ask them and they did not want to be the ones to tell him, neither did they want to lie to him.

I watched them go in to see him all day long. I watched them play the "Everything is fine" game when everyone, including Joe, knew better. Finally that evening I waited until after the brief visitation time allowed in intensive care. There was a wonderful nurse there who was willing to tell me the truth about his condition. She said she did not have the right to tell him, but if he asked she would do so anyway.

I stepped into the room and Joe said, "Doug, I want to know." I have had the task of telling people about their condition before, but I never had done so for someone so close. My knees shook all the time I was telling him. When it was over, I had to go off and cry, but I gave my uncle the wonderful gift of dying ritual.

When the family was allowed back in, the atmosphere was completely different. I had written Joe a letter and he asked the immediate family to gather around his bed while I read it to him. We all had the chance to tell Joe how much we loved him. He had the chance to tell us how much he loved us. His older brother kissed him and, all the way home, kept saying, "I would not have missed tonight for anything in the world." That is dying ritual. It is only possible when we can get past our fear of death and break out of the prison of the positive.

Alzheimer's patients must have this experience earlier than the rest of us, but it is still possible. When the diagnosis comes, the tendency is to lock ourselves into the positive prison. We dare not talk about the disease. We must keep it happy at all times. Our efforts to "protect" our loved ones can lock them away from some wonderful experiences and joy.

What we need is a new concept of death. Something to let us see death as passage into life. Something to give us enough hope for the future that we will not see death as the worst thing that could ever happen to someone.

There was a cartoon in *The New York Times* one year at Easter that showed a group of caterpillars carrying a cocoon out for burial. The caterpillars were dressed in black and were sad. There was a butterfly up in the corner of the cartoon. The caption read, "What the caterpillar calls the end, God calls a butterfly." We need something like that.

I found a new concept. I wish I had written it, but I did not do so. I have not even been able to find out who did write it, so we will just have to give credit to some wonderful, but anonymous, writer.

The Parable Of The Twins

Once upon a time twin boys were conceived in the same womb. Weeks passed and the twins developed. As their awareness grew, they laughed for joy: "Isn't it great that we were conceived? Isn't it great to be alive?"

Together the twins explored their world. When they found their mother's cord that gave them life, they sang for joy: "How great is our mother's love that she shares her own life with us!"

As weeks stretched into months the twins noticed how much each was changing. "What does it mean?" asked the one. "It means that our stay in this world is drawing to an end." said the other one. "But I don't want to go," said the other one. "I want to stay here always." "We have no choice," said the other. "But maybe there is life after birth!" "But how can there be?" responded the one. " We will shed our life cord, and how is life possible without it? Besides, we have seen evidence that others were here before us, and none of them have returned to tell us that there is life after birth. No, this is the end."

And so the one fell into deep despair, saying, "If conception ends in birth, what is the purpose of life in the womb? It's meaningless! Maybe there is no mother after all." "But there has to be," protested the other. "How else did we get here? How do we remain alive?"

"Have you ever seen our mother?" said the one. "Maybe she lives only in our minds. Maybe we made her up because the idea made us feel good."

And so the last days in the womb were filled with deep questioning and fear. Finally, the moment of birth arrived.

When the twins had passed from their world, they opened their eyes and they cried. For what they saw exceeded their fondest dreams.

I Corinthians 2:9
"Eye has not seen
Ear has not heard
Nor has it so much
As dawned on man
What God had prepared
For those who love Him."

Chapter XII

Have A Resurrection

When my father died I did not feel anything. He died holding my hand and I was numb. I did not shed a tear through the whole funeral experience. People came to express condolences and I thanked them while I saw no need for their concern. I made all of the funeral arrangements and took care of every detail, but I felt not one hint of sorrow.

At first, I thought I was in shock over the death. I have written about the fact that, even though we expect the death and often pray that it will come to relieve suffering, when it comes we are in shock. I thought this was what was happening to me and that the shock would wear off in a few weeks.

When the shock did not wear off, I decided I had already done my grieving during the illness. After all, I had gone through the gradual loss of everything about my father that I held dear.

His personality died long before his body stopped breathing. He had been one of the funniest people I had ever known. He never met a stranger. He was held in such high esteem by so many people because of his delightfully funny persona. That all passed and he almost completely stopped talking. The nearer he got to death, the less he talked. Some folks find it too hard to say goodbye so they just divorce themselves from the family. Silence becomes their protector. My father divorced.

When I became "parent" to my father, our communication died. I had no idea that would happen or that it happens to others. He came to me for some advice and, from that night on, our world was strained. He would not come to our house unless he just had to do so. I would not go see him unless I had some other place I needed to be in a few moments so I would not have to stay long. We had gone from being best friends to uncomfortable strangers, and we both suffered the loss of communication.

His illness took away all of the happy times we shared. Once we loved to drive around and talk. When I took him riding now his illness totally dominated the conversation.

The pressure of providing care made him seem like more of a burden than I ever wanted or expected. How could I possibly consider him to be a burden?

I had already lost my father by the time his body died. What was left to grieve? I felt nothing and thought the lack of feelings meant I had already done my grieving. Then about eight months after his death I woke up in the night reliving the day he died, and my grieving began.

I now understand that when a loved one dies after a long illness, quite often the caregiver does not grieve at first. We are too exhausted to grieve. We have no emotions left with which to grieve. The long-term depression has left us emotionally flat and we do not feel anything. For some of us it takes about eight months to recover enough for the grieving to begin.

This delayed reaction can cause some people to feel a great deal of guilt. They, like me, wonder if they just did not love the person. Maybe I really did not care as much as I thought I did. When my grief finally came, I felt a great sense of relief and release from guilt.

Since I had no feelings when he died I did not care whether or not we even had a funeral. I knew we needed one for my mother's sake, but I could not work up any interest at all. Eight months later when the grief came, the memories of the funeral were a great comfort to me. I needed to relive that experience and it helped me establish his significance and realize that he was significant to others. The memory of the care people showed and the wonderful tributes they voiced about my father were great helps in meeting my need for significance.

At the time of his death, I did not care
whether or not I saw his body. When the grief
came, and I awoke in the night, my first vision
was of my father in the process of dying. He
was like a little bird that had fallen out of the
nest and lay on the ground peeping but making
no sound. Dad's mouth would open and close
but no air passed. The only thing that could
replace that memory was the memory of how
natural and peaceful he looked at the funeral.
I hear folks say they want to remember their
loved one the way they were and not in some
casket. That is fine if you do not have to see
them after they are ill. I treasure the vision of
my last view of my father.

Recently, a family called on me to officiate at
the funeral of their father. They said they
wanted the very simplest of funerals. After all,
he had Alzheimer's and the disease had long ago
taken him away. He was old and most of his
friends were gone. How meaningful could a
funeral be?

When my grandmother died, my father said,
"Let's go down and visit Momma Hoyle." We sat
by her body in the funeral home and began
telling stories about her. Those stories are told
again and again and, as long as they are told,
she will be alive in us. No one is dead until they
are forgotten, and she will never be forgotten as
long as we live.

That experience has led me over the years to meet with the family the night before the funeral for a time of story telling. These are never morbid times. We laugh together and cry together and remember the life of a loved one. When I asked this family to have such a meeting, they were not sure how valuable such a time could be. He was old and had Alzheimer's.

The stories began slowly, but gradually they began to flow. "Do you remember the time he fell off of the windmill?" "Remember the time we all went camping and everything went wrong?" "Remember how mad he got when he caught all of us smoking behind the barn?" That old man came alive among us. We had ourselves a resurrection. He no longer had Alzheimer's. He was no longer old. He was alive and we were there to celebrate his life.

When the time comes to say goodbye to your loved one, my prayer is that you, too, will have a resurrection. That your loved one will come back to life among you and you will celebrate everything that life meant.

A Place To Journal

Two of my aunts took care of my grandfather for five years before he died. He was ninety-eight when he died and was not an easy patient to care for. He was almost stone deaf, and cantankerous would be too mild a word for his personality. They were able to give the care largely because of their delightful sense of humor.

From the day he died, they have never ceased to tell the stories of the caregiving days. Some are sad. Some are inspirational. Some are fall-down laughing funny. They remember so many of these experiences and they have great meaning for them. They also have forgotten so many of the really good ones.

For the sake of memory, and because it is healing to write down the experiences we have, I am leaving several pages for you to journal. If you do not have one specific place to collect the stories, you probably will not write them down. I hope you will keep this little book handy and write down the good, the bad, and the memorable things that happen during the walk through this lonesome valley.

A Chronology Of The Disease

Section IV

Resource Section

Finding help in the valley

A Chronology Of The Disease

Sayings To Remember

Poignant Moments

•

The Funny Times

Things I Learned While Giving Care

.

Special People Who Walked With Me
Through My Lonesome Valley

Selected Resources from In-Sight Books
by Doug Manning

Grief
Don't Take My Grief Away From Me
The Gift of Significance
The Special Care Series
Lean On Me Gently–Helping the Grieving Child
Thoughts for the Lonely Nights *journal and CD*
Thoughts for the Grieving Christian *journal and CD*
The Funeral
Thoughts for the Holidays

Elder Care
Aging is a Family Affair
Parenting Our Parents
Searching for Normal Feelings
Share My Lonesome Valley–The Slow Grief of Long-Term Care
Socks–How to Solve Problems
Visiting in a Nursing Home
When Love Gets Tough–Making the Nursing Home Decision

Other Resources from In-Sight Books
I Know Someone Who Died coloring book *by Connie Manning*
The Empty Chair–The Journey of Grief After
Suicide *by Beryl Glover*
The Shattered Dimension–The Journey of Grief After
Suicide video *by Beryl Glover*
Comfort Cards *bereavement card collection*

For a complete catalog or ordering information contact:
In-Sight Books, Inc.
1-800-658-9262 or 405-810-9501
www.insightbooks.com

Organizations

You can contact these national organizations to obtain information on support groups, educational materials and other research that might be helpful in your caregiving.

National Alzheimer's Association
919 N Michigan Avenue
Suite 1000
Chicago, IL 60611
312-335-8700
800-272-3900
www.alz.org

Alzheimer's Disease Education and Referral Center (ADEAR)
P O Box 8250
Silver Spring, MD 20907
800-438-4380
www.alzheimers.org

American Cancer Society
1599 Clifton Road, NE
Atlanta, GA 30329
404-320-3333
800-ACS-2345
www.cancer.org

American Heart Association
7272 Greenville Avenue
Dallas, TX 75231
800-AHA-USA1
www.amhrt.org

National Stroke Association
96 Inverness Drive East, Suite 1
Englewood, CO 80112-5112
303-649-1552
www.stroke.org

National Hospice Organization
1901 N Moore Street
Suite 901
Arlington, VA 22209
703-243-5900
www.nho.org

AIDS Information Network
1211 Chestnut Street
7th Floor
Philadelphia, PA 19107
215-575-1110

ALS Association National Office
21021 Ventura Blvd
Suite 321
Woodland Hills, CA 91364
818-340-7500
www.alsa.org

American Lung Association
1740 Broadway
New York, NY 10019-4374
212-315-8700
www.lungusa.org

American Parkinson Disease Association
1250 Hylan Blvd, Suite 4B
Staten Island, NY 10305-1946
800-223-2732

National Institute on Aging
Bldg 31, Room 5C27
31 Center Dr MSC 2292
Bethesda, MD   20892
301-496-1752
www.nia.nih.gov

National Family Caregivers Association
10400 Connecticut Ave #500
Kensington, MD   20895
800-896-3650
info@nfcacares.org
www.nfcacares.org

Gilda's Club (Cancer Support)
195 W Houston Street
New York, NY   10014
212-647-9700

Leukemia Society of America
600 Third Ave
New York, NY   10016
212-573-8484

Multiple Sclerosis Association of America
706 Haddonfield Road
Cherry Hill, NJ   08002
800-833-4672

American Brain Tumor Association
2720 River Road, Suite 146
Des Plaines IL   60018
800-886-2282